I0706625

YOU ARE THE BEST!

REAL LOVE

I LOVE YOU

XOXO

CUTIE PIE

CUP CAKE

FEBRUARY

SWEET PEA

YOU AND ME

I LOVE YOU

HUG ME

ALL MINE

BE TRUE

SUN SHINE!

ONE I LOVE

TO MY SWEET GODSON
HAPPY VALENTINE'S DAY!
COLORING CARD

Copyright 2018
by Florabella Publishing, LLC
All rights reserved. No part of this book may be reproduced in any form or by any electronic or mechanical means including information storage and retrieval systems, without permission in writing from the authors. The only exception is by a reviewer, who may quote short excerpts in a review.

YOU'RE SWEET

Thank you for your recent purchase! We hope you've enjoyed your Valentine Coloring Card.

Happy Valentine's Day!

From florabella publishing

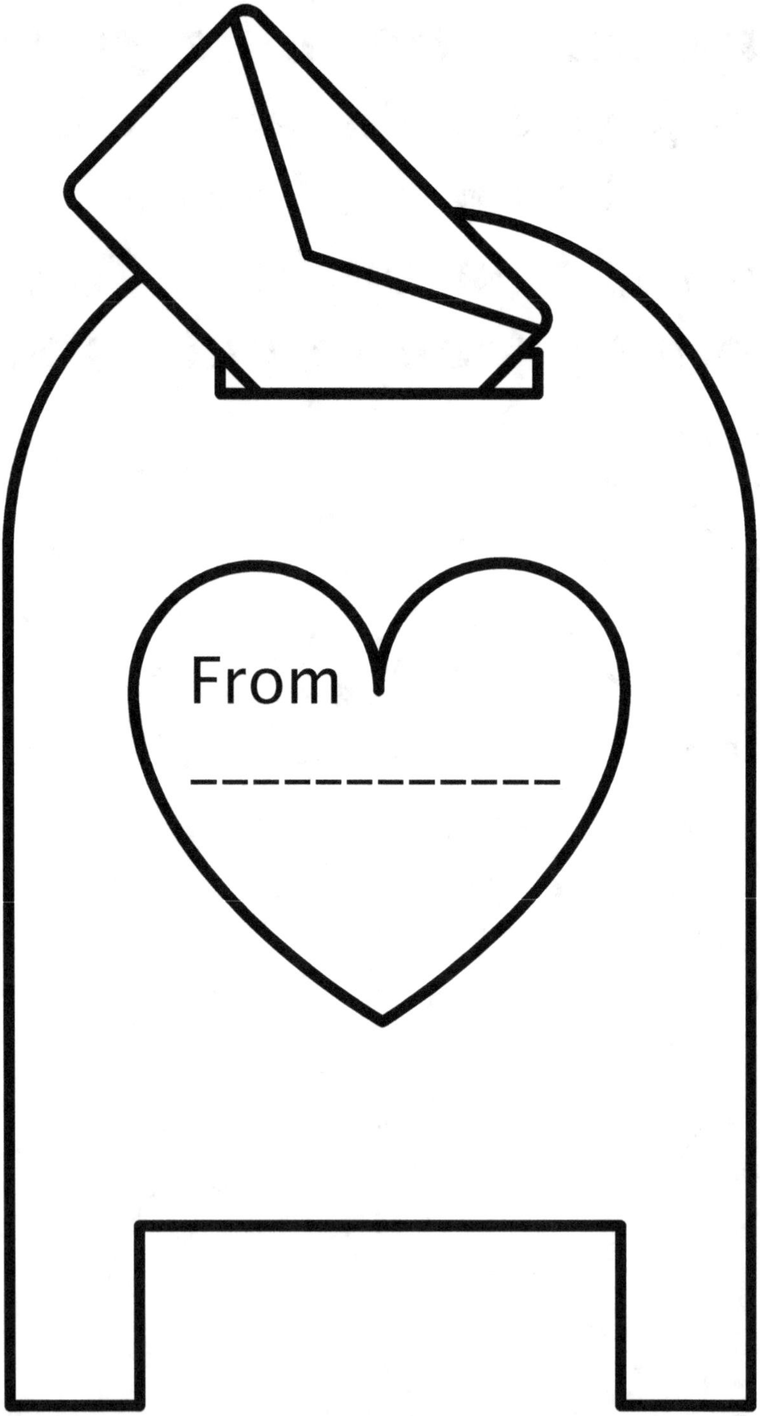
From

www.ingramcontent.com/pod-product-compliance
Lightning Source LLC
Chambersburg PA
CBHW071021260726
48662CB00022B/987
* 9 7 8 1 9 8 3 6 2 6 7 7 7 *